The crazy CHRISTMAS joke book

2019

!U19

The crazy CHRISTMAS joke book

PUFFIN

PUFFIN BOOKS

Published by the Penguin Group
Penguin Books Ltd, 80 Strand, London WC2R 0RL, England
Penguin Group (USA), Inc., 375 Hudson Street, New York, New York 10014, USA
Penguin Books Australia Ltd, 250 Camberwell Road, Camberwell, Victoria 3124, Australia
Penguin Books Canada Ltd, 10 Alcorn Avenue, Toronto, Ontario, Canada M4V 3B2
Penguin Books India (P) Ltd, 11 Community Centre, Panchsheel Park,
New Delhi – 110 017, India
Penguin Group (NZ), cnr Airborne and Rosedale Roads, Albany, Auckland 1310, New Zealand
Penguin Books (South Africa) (Pty) Ltd, 24 Sturdee Avenue, Rosebank 2196, South Africa

Penguin Books Ltd, Registered Offices: 80 Strand, London WC2R 0RL, England

www.penguin.com

First published as *The Little Christmas Joke Book* in Puffin Books 2002
Published in this edition as *The Crazy Christmas Joke Book* in 2004
007

Copyright © Puffin Books, 2002
Illustrations copyright © Nick Stearn, 2002

The moral right of the illustrator has been asserted

Made and printed in England by Clays Ltd, St Ives plc

British Library Cataloguing in Publication Data
A CIP catalogue record for this book is available from the British Library

ISBN 978-0-14-131871-4

www.greenpenguin.co.uk

MIX
Paper from
responsible sources
FSC
www.fsc.org   FSC™ C018179

Penguin Books is committed to a sustainable
future for our business, our readers and our planet.
This book is made from Forest Stewardship
Council™ certified paper.

ALWAYS LEARNING   **PEARSON**

Silly Santas

Who carries Santa's books?

His books elf.

Who brings presents to crows at Christmas?

Santa Caws.

1

What sort of mobile phone has Santa got?

Pay as you ho, ho, ho.

What do you get if you cross
Santa with a flying saucer?

A UF ho, ho, ho.

What do you get if you cross Santa
with a gardener?

Someone who likes to hoe, hoe, hoe.

What do you call people who
are afraid of Santa Claus?

Claustrophobic.

What do you call a smelly Santa?

Farta Christmas.

Why does Father Christmas cry a lot?

Because he gets a little
santamental.

How does Santa take his photos?
With his North Pole-aroid.

What does Father Christmas do
when his elves misbehave?

He gives them the sack.

toys

Christmas Crackers

What did one angel say to the other?

'Halo there.'

What are brown and creep around the house?

Mince spies.

What did one Christmas tree
say to the other?

'I've got a present fir you.'

What does Dracula write on
his Christmas cards?
'Best vicious
of the season'

What does Father Christmas write
on his Christmas cards?

'ABCDEFGHIJKMNOPQRSTUVWXYZ (No-L!!)'

How does Good King Wenceslas
like his pizzas?

Deep pan, crisp and even.

What do ducks do before
Christmas dinner?

Pull their Christmas quackers.

What do you get when you cross an archer
with a gift wrapper?

Ribbon Hood.

 8

thanks, santa!

Did you know that Father Christmas only comes once a year because it takes him the other 364 days to read all the grateful e-mails he gets from his satisfied customers? Well, that's what he told us – and here are some of them to prove it . . .

From: The Snowman
To: Father Christmas

The round-the-world ticket was a nice idea, but I've pretty much been there, done that. Can I get a refund?

From: The Mummy
To: Santa

Thanks for the designer bandages – they are the business. I will keep them under wraps until my next film premiere.

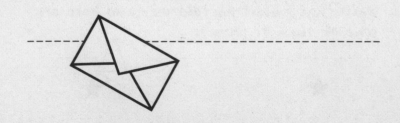

From: The Fairy at the Top of the Christmas
Tree
To: Father Christmas

I'm very grateful for the new pair of wings.
However, I've been stuck up here so long that I
don't know how to use them. Could I have flying
lessons next year?

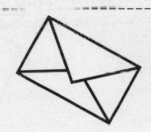

From: 007
To: Santa

Thank you for the book *Secret Codes and How to
Crack Them*. I noticed, however, that you
addressed the package to 'James Pond'. Please
note for future reference that the name is Bond
— James Bond.

From: The Loch Ness Monster
To: Santa

Wot no presents again? I've really got
the hump now.

From: Dracula
To: Santa

Fangs a lot for the tooth-whitening
kit. My glow-in-the-dark molars are
making a great impression on the
ladies.

From: The Invisible Man
To: Santa

The book *How to Tell Really Convincing
Lies* was just what I wanted. But when I
tried it out on my friends it didn't
work. They said they could see right
through me.

From: An alien life form
To: Santa

Dear Santa

I'm grateful for the cosy gloves you
sent for Christmas. Unfortunately, I
have fifty-seven fingers. Could you
bear this in mind for next year – a
few more pairs would come in very
handy.

Hey Santa!

TOO MANY COOKIES BY THE FIRESIDE?
TROUSERS FEELING TIGHT?

Get into peak physical condition for the New Year with our state-of-the-art Chimney-climbing Simulator. Regular use of the ChimMaster will enable even the chubbiest of Santas to get trim in a trice. Contains the following features:

*Anti-slip insides
* Authentic birds nests
* Real soot
(plus pack of
freshen-up wipes)

KNOCK KNOCK!

'Knock knock.'
'Who's there?'
'Rabbit.'
'Rabbit who?'
'Rabbit up neatly, it's a present.'

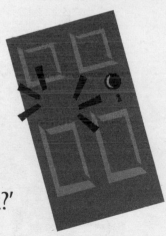

'Knock knock.'
'Who's there?'
'Arthur.'
'Arthur who?'
'Arthur any mince pies left?'

'Knock knock.'
'Who's there?'
'Wendy.'
'Wendy who?'
'Wendy red red robin comes bob bob bobbin along.'

'Knock knock.'
'Who's there?'
'Wenceslas.'
'Wenceslas who?'
'Wenceslas bus home?'

'Knock knock.'
'Who's there?'
'Wayne.'
'Wayne who?'
'Wayne in a manger!'

'Knock knock.'
'Who's there?'
'Doughnut.'
'Doughnut who?'
'Doughnut open till Christmas Day!'

'Knock knock.'
'Who's there?'
'Avery.'
'Avery who?'
'Avery merry Christmas!'

'Knock knock.'
'Who's there?'
'Holly.'
'Holly who?'
'Holly-days are here again!'

'Knock knock.'
'Who's there?'
'Police.'
'Police who?'
'Police don't make me eat all my Brussels sprouts!'

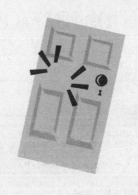

'Knock knock.'
'Who's there?'
'Wanda.'
'Wanda who?'
'Wanda know what you're getting for Christmas?'

TOP TEN EXCUSES FOR FORGETTING TO BUY SOMEONE A PRESENT

I put it in a safe place and now I can't find it.

I've donated it to charity – isn't that what you wanted?

I thought I could get it cheaper in the sales.

I couldn't think of anything to buy for a person who has everything.

Practical Jokes to Play on FatherChristmas

Instead of putting out mince pies and sherry, leave him a glass of water, a piece of bread and a note saying you heard he was on a diet.

Leave him a note saying you've gone away and could he let the cat out and feed the goldfish.

Leave him a note saying his wife phoned to remind him to pick up the kids from school on his way home.

Decorate your house for Hallowe'en and play a tape recording of someone saying 'trick or treat' and laughing sinisterly.

Leave him a note saying that he must have a permit to park on your roof and that unauthorized sledges will be clamped.

festive food

What's the most popular wine at Christmas?
'Do I have to eat these Brussels sprouts?'

Who beats his chest and swings from
Christmas cake to Christmas cake?
Tarzipan!

'Mum, can I have a dog for Christmas?'
'No, you can have turkey like everyone else!'

'Dad, will the Christmas pudding be long?'
'No, silly, it'll be round!'

What's the best thing to put into a
Christmas cake?
Your teeth!

What do you drain your
Christmas Brussels sprouts with?
An advent colander!

What do vampires put on their turkey at
Christmas?
Grave-y!

What happens if you eat the
Christmas-tree decorations?
You get tinsel-itus!

Who is never hungry at Christmas?
The turkey – he's always stuffed!

Say No to Your Glo!

Is embarrassing redness getting you down?

Try Blushaway, the fantastic miracle cream. Just one application and you can wave goodbye to your facial flushes. No more teasing, no more jokes – just the confidence that comes with knowing you ain't glowing.

TEN THINGS THAT WOULD MAKE CHRISTMAS EVEN BETTER THAN IT IS NOW

1: Presents that you actually like

2: Extra-long Christmas stockings

3: The ability to eat as much chocolate as you want without feeling sick

4: An immediate ban on Brussels sprouts

5: No grannies (or similar) allowed to kiss you

6: Genuinely funny cracker jokes

7: No repeats on TV – and no showing of _The Great Escape_

8: Endless supplies of batteries for all the presents that need them

9: Relatives who don't cheat at games

10: A magic fairy to write all your thank-you letters for you

Bestselling Books

MAKE YOUR PARENTS GET WHAT YOU WANT — *Ruth Lesschild*

SLEDGING FOR BEGINNERS — I.C. BOTTOM

THE BIG CHRISTMAS QUIZ BOOK — I. DUNNOE AND NOAH LITTLE

101 Cures for Indigestion — IVOR PAIN

What to do after Christmas Dinner Clare Inup

at Christmas

How to Get the Perfect Gift — B. GOOD

Disappointing Gifts — M. T. BOX

PREDICT YOUR PRESENTS by P. KING

WINNING AT CHARADES VIC TREE

The Art of Kissing — Miss L. Toe

Christmas Creatures

What do elephants sing at Christmas?

'No-elephants, No-elephants!'

What do angry mice send to
each other at Christmas?

Cross-mouse cards!

How do sheep greet each other at Christmas?

'A merry Christmas to ewe.'

What's very scary and squeaks?

The Ghost of Christmouse Past.

What do you call a cat on a beach at Christmas?
Sandy Claws.

What kind of bird can write?
A PENguin.

Why do birds fly south for the winter?
Because it's too far to walk.

Where do polar bears vote?
The North Poll.

What did the sheep say to Santa?

'Season's Bleatings.'

What do you call a polar bear wearing earmuffs?

Anything you want. He can't hear you.

What do reindeer have that no other animals in the world have?

Baby reindeer.

Why did the turkey cross the road?

To prove he wasn't a chicken.

Dear Deerdre

The straight-talking deer,
who tells it like it is.

Dear Deerdre,

All the other deer laugh at me! What can I do?

Rudolph

Look, mate, you may have a bit of a rosy hooter but, let's face it, you're famous. Someone's even gone and written a song about you. So stop feeling so sorry for yourself — nobody else does.

Deerdre
xx

Dear Deerdre,

Sometimes I wonder if it is all worth it. All year round nobody wants to know me and I'm all alone without a friend in the world – just a few reindeers for company. But then December arrives and suddenly hundreds of children turn up at my grotto demanding to know what they're getting for Christmas. I don't know if I can cope with the stress any more.

Santa

Dear Santa,

Well, you read the job description, didn't you? You should count yourself lucky; you only work one night every year. Cut the complaining and get on with it.

Dear Deerdre,

I am a top TV chef, and every year I tell the viewers how to make their own Christmas puddings, cake, mince pies and even how to cook a turkey lunch with all the trimmings. I am getting really bored with it. Why can't they remember how to cook all these things themselves?

Top TV chef

Dear Top TV chef,

What a waste of time – just tell the viewers to go to the supermarket and BUY the stuff like everyone else does. Duh!

Deerdre
xx

Dear Deerdre,

I am one of Santa's helpful elves. I used to enjoy my job, but things have been very difficult at the workshop recently. If I get the presents mixed up, Santa shouts at me. Lately I find myself, sniff, just bursting into tears whenever it happens.

Elf Number 75

You've definitely got low elf-esteem. Find out how to deal with your bothersome boss by buying my brilliant new book, *Sort it, Santa!* priced £6.99 and available from all good bookshops.

Deerdre
xx

it's game time!

What game do crocodiles like?

Snap!

What is a ghost's favourite game?

Moan-opoly.

Why do rude people always
lose at Scrabble?

Because they don't mind
their Ps and Qs.

What game do
snakes always win?

Twister.

Why did the jigsaw get upset?

It was going to pieces.

Why should you never play
games in the jungle?

Because there are some
terrible cheetahs there.

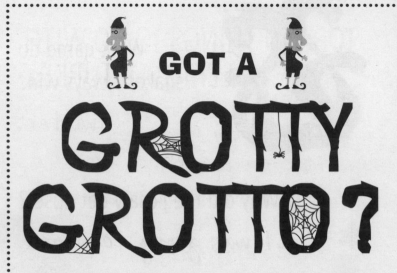

GOT A GROTTY GROTTO?

Who could blame all you working Santas out there? Chimney soot on your clothes, reindeer poo everywhere – and you've got millions of children to deal with in a single night. It's no wonder you can't find the time to clean up.

So if you need a helping hand, just call

ELVES Я US

OUR HORDES OF FAIRY FRIENDS WILL GET TO GRIPS WITH YOUR GRIME IN NO TIME!

TOP TEN THINGS TO DO WITH LEFTOVER TURKEY

1. Make turkey sandwiches
2. Make turkey curry
3. Make turkey casserole
4. Make turkey salad
5. Make turkey stir-fry
6. Make turkey omelette
7. Make turkey pancakes
8. Make turkey surprise
9. Shout at entire family for making vomiting noises whenever the word 'turkey' is mentioned
10. Order pizzas

The UNWANTED Gift Spell

Instructions

1. Select suspect package from under tree. (Likely to have 'Love from Granny/Auntie' tag attached. If gift feels squidgy, it may well be an article of clothing. In which case, have no doubts about casting this spell.)

2. Take your wand and wave over gift while reciting the following verse.

O lurking parcel, o dodgy gift,
May you change your shape and shift
Into something more top of the range.
It's always nice to have a change.
Lo! what lies beneath your exterior
will no longer be inferior.

3. Proceed to unwrap gift with cries of joy.
(If the spell hasn't worked, bad luck. Try again next year.)

santa's little helpers

What do the elves sing to Santa Claus?

'Freeze a Jolly Good Fellow.'

What do elves write on
their Christmas cards?

'Wishing you a fairy
merry Christmas!'

Why did the elf put his bed
near the fireplace?

He wanted to sleep like a log.

What do elves learn at school?

The elf-a-bet.

Where do Santa's helpers go to relax?

An elf farm.

Why did Santa tell off one of the elves?

Because he was goblin his
Christmas dinner.

TOP TEN CHRISTMAS PRESENTS FOR DADS

1
Socks

2
More socks

3
Socks again

4
Even more socks

5
Just for a change – socks

6
Christmas-themed socks

7
'Comedy' socks

8
Christmas-themed comedy socks

9
A two-pair pack of Christmas-themed comedy socks

10
Slippers in the shape of bear's feet

Top Ten Things you *don't* want to find in your Christmas stocking

1. A massive hole
2. A note from Father Christmas saying he's sorry he didn't get round to doing the Christmas shopping but he'll buy you something in the sales instead
3. A mouldy satsuma
4. A CD of 'Crackin' Christmas Hits to Sing Along To!'
5. A big hairy spider hiding in the toe
6. A 'hilarious' Santa hat and beard that you'll have to wear all day to keep your family happy
7. Anything that's useful for school
8. Dodgy plastic toys that always break immediately
9. 'Fun' flashing Christmas-tree earrings (especially if you're a boy)
10. A packet of 'Thank You' cards

Chilly Chuckles

What is an ig?

An igloo without the toilet.

Why is it so cold at Christmas?

Because it's in Decembrrrrr!

What do snowmen have for breakfast?

Snowflakes.

What do snow children have for breakfast?

Ice Krispies.

What do you get if you cross a snowman with a vampire?

Frostbite.

What did one snowman say to the other?

'Ice to see you.'

Why does Buffy like snow?

Because she's an excellent sleigher.

What's Santa's favourite Chinese food?

Stir-fried ice and chilly sauce.

Cracking Carols

We three Kings of Orient are.
One in a taxi,
One in a car,
One on a scooter beeping his hooter,
Following yonder star.

Good King Wenceslas looked out,

On the feast of Stephen.

A snowball hit him on the snout,

And made it all uneven.

Brightly shone his conk that night,

Though the pain was cruel,

Till a doctor came in sight,

Riding on a mule (mu-oooh-el).

HEY, TURKEYS!

Don't be a dull stay-at-home bird. Get away from it all this year with a fabulous winter break, where you can fluff up your feathers and put some pizzazz into your plumage!

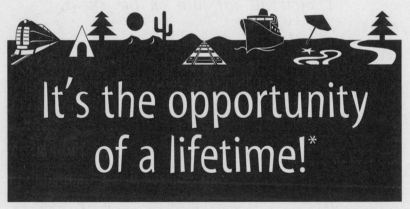

It's the opportunity of a lifetime!*

Departures 20 December – 1 January

* Listen, turkeys, this will be the ONLY opportunity in your lifetime so we strongly advise taking up this offer . . .

Have a Tricky Christmas

Here's some easy Christmas magic to impress your family and friends.

Coin it in!

What you need:

A pound coin (Preferably from an audience member!)

A dark handkerchief

A partner in crime (You might have to share the pound with them.)

Trick: Get a pound from an audience member and show it around in the palm of your hand, then cover it with a dark handkerchief. Ask some friends to reach under the handkerchief, one at a time, to confirm that the coin is still there. After the last person has done this, ask someone to take away the handkerchief. The coin has gone!

Method: Hold out your hand with the coin on it and drape the handkerchief over it. The last person to check the coin is the one you have previously asked to secretly help you. He or she just takes away the coin! This is usually quite easy to organize, as most people will go along with the trick just to see the effect on their friends and family!

Mind-reader

What you need:
A selection of different objects (Christmas presents would work well.)
A partner in crime

Trick: You tell your audience that you will leave the room, then come back in and magically read their minds to say which object they have chosen while you were outside. You then walk out of the room and your assistant picks Granny (or whoever) to select one object in the room. You return and are able to say what that object is. It's magic!

Method:

Before you start your performance, you need to decide on a secret object with your assistant. When you return to the room, the assistant points to a couple of different objects and asks you if Gran picked it or not. You say no and, after a few goes, the assistant points to the secret object that you picked previously. This gives you the signal that the next object your assistant points to will be the one chosen by Gran.

You can have a lot of fun with this one and can even have more than one person picking different things (although you'll have to pick more than one secret object).

festive fun

What do you get in December that you don't get in any other month?

The letter 'D'.

Why didn't the skeleton go to the Christmas party?

He had no body to go with.

What do skunks sing at Christmas?

'*Jingle Smells*'

What did Adam say the day before Christmas?

'*It's Christmas, Eve.*'

Which deer has the worst table manners?

Rude-olph.

What do you get if you cross
an insect with a reindeer?

Antlers.

THE BARMY BOOK CLUB CHRISTMAS PICKS

SPOOKY HOUSES OF BRITAIN

HUGO FIRST

STARRED CHOICE

CHINESE GOLF

HO LIN WON

FOR SPORTS FANS!

PLAY BETTER FOOTBALL

MR GOAL

it's snow joke

What do you tell a
stressed-out snowman?

'Chill out!'

What do you call a snowman in July?
A puddle.

What's a snowman's favourite
Mexican food?
Brrrr-itos!

What's the least exciting animal
at the North Pole?

A polar bore.

What sort of insects
love snow?

Mo-ski-toes.

What do you get if you cross
The Snowman with a mobile phone?

'We're Talking in the Air . . .'

Potty Presents

Why did Scrooge buy everyone budgies for Christmas?

Because they were going cheep.

What did the dog get for Christmas?

A mobile bone.

Why couldn't the cat work
her new DVD player?

She kept pressing 'Paws'.

What did the farmer get for Christmas?

A cow-culator.

Why did Dracula want
mouthwash for Christmas?

To get rid of his bat breath.

What do DJs love about Christmas?

Doing all their rapping on Christmas Eve.

What do witches use to wrap up their presents?

Spell-otape

What did the spider want for Christmas?

A book of all the latest web sites.

WHAT TO DO WITH YOUR UNWANTED GIFTS

Got a load of peculiar presents for Christmas? Don't worry, simply follow the instructions below and put that present to another use:

UNWANTED GIFT 1
A rubbish CD by a band you hate
SOLUTION: Use as a stylish drinks 'coaster' or make a hole in it and hang on the tree as a shiny decoration.

UNWANTED GIFT 2
'Fun' flashing Christmas novelty socks
SOLUTION: Keep hidden under your bed in case there is ever a power cut. Or put them to use if your fairy lights cut out.

 UNWANTED GIFT 3

Disgusting toiletries that you wouldn't touch with a barge pole

SOLUTION: Save till next year and give to a relative who has no sense of smell.

UNWANTED GIFT 4

A dodgy scarf and hat set

SOLUTION: Save it to adorn your next snowman. Or unravel and use for string.

UNWANTED GIFT 5

A really dull jigsaw puzzle

SOLUTION: Use the pieces to prop up a wonky table or chair. Or give it to your little brother/sister to keep them quiet for a bit (only don't tell them there's a piece missing).

The All-purpose Thank-you Letter

Save time after Christmas with our fantastic instant thank-you letter! Simply choose the words that apply and delete the rest. Hey presto!

Dear (insert name)

....

Thank you for the lovely gift/present/
card/thingamajig/as yet unidentified
object.

It is extremely useful/attractive/
unusual/dull/horrible and I am sure
it will come in very useful for a special
occasion/school trip/holiday/car-boot
sale/charity shop.*

It was very kind/generous/nice/
surprising/odd of you to think of me
this Christmas.

Yours sincerely
(insert your name)

....

* Or I can always give it to someone else next year.

Have a Happy Ho-Ho Holiday!